Australia
a Migrant Experience

by
Martin Kari

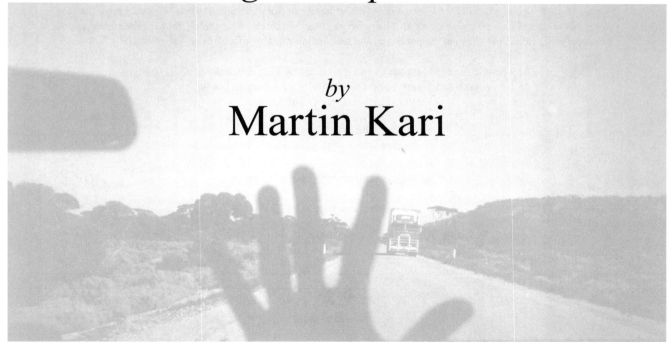

Interior Graphics/Art Credit: Martin Kari

Balboa Press books may be ordered through booksellers or by contacting:

Balboa Press
A Division of Hay House
1663 Liberty Drive
Bloomington, IN 47403
www.balboapress.com
1 (877) 407-4847

Because of the dynamic nature of the Internet, any web addresses or links contained in this book may have changed since publication and may no longer be valid. The views expressed in this work are solely those of the author and do not necessarily reflect the views of the publisher, and the publisher hereby disclaims any responsibility for them.

Any people depicted in stock imagery provided by Thinkstock are models, and such images are being used for illustrative purposes only.
Certain stock imagery © Thinkstock.

ISBN: 978-1-5043-1233-2 (sc)
ISBN: 978-1-5043-1234-9 (e)

Print information available on the last page.

Balboa Press rev. date: 02/22/2018

BALBOA
PRESS
A DIVISION OF HAY HOUSE

About the Author

Born during World War II in Transylvania, the author undertook many directions in his life, starting as a refugee in Germany. Historically speaking, war had dwindled the family in the past.

As a survivor, the author firstly went through technical and then formal higher education, with the intention of, with his family, going out into the world to learn real-life issues. As an 'Aussie' living Down-Under for the last twenty-five years, the author envisages a return to grassroots from whence we should act with common sense in life. It would be a 'mission impossible' to make a summary here.

Dedications

My thoughts are dedicated to my family.

Contents

Introduction

About Migration

Throughout history, and nature, migration has been a phenomenon, and one that includes all living forms on our planet.

Some species show regular patterns of movements within nature's cycles, cycles that were developed over a long period of time in order to survive; the migration of birds and whales all takes place before winter sets in.

What about human beings? How do we respond to migration as a mean for survival?

Only a few Nomads known in Africa, Asia, and small pockets within the northern Arctic Circle, still roam today over areas that are becoming increasingly smaller through civilisation. The days of migration over vast continental areas are gone in today's world. Indeed, throughout history, migration on a grand scale sometimes was the catalyst, the trigger for hostile actions amongst peoples—Dschingis- Khan's exodus and Alexander the Great are good examples. One only need examine the contributions of Greece, Rome and Europe in the quest for colonisation.

Today, the economic status of a society, together with its social achievements are the guarantors of a settled, stable society. Those societies less stable in nature are often drawn to the benefits of a more established and economically sound community. For purposes of this discussion, perhaps it's useful to think in terms of 'camps' and schools of thought, that might consider migration as a means to achieve a 'switch' to a more thriving society or conversely opting to follow more austere directions. The establishment of more simplified existence often proves to be a powerful siren song for some—pursuit of a 'back to the basics'. There are many motivating factors for a migration from one camp to another;

sometimes the desire to do so is powerful enough to overcome the restrictions and collective desire imposed by a country or camp.

Migrant family:
From left—Mirja, Raija, Risto, Peter, Arja, and Martin in Frankfurt

As economic situations in all societies are subject to fluctuations, it is reasonable to suggest that processes like migration should be also subject to fluctuations; fluctuations permitting a society to self-regulate. In that vein, it is a natural progression for a society to regulate their own affairs according to their needs.

Officially, today there is mainly one country remaining as a migration destination, at present—Australia. Canada has changed officially its status as a migration country.

Personal experience consisted of forced migration through World War II from Transylvania and professional migration to South Africa and Brazil, which took place on a voluntary basis during my life. The decision to migrate to Australia in 1981 was the result of considerations borne of those experiences, combined with a good deal of renewed hope and expectations.

I do not debate here my two professional migrations before the Australian decision; however, they have undoubtedly influenced this, my last migration decision. The decision to migrate from Europe to a distant country like Australia is by no means an everyday decision. I believe therefore, due to the weightiness of such an endeavour, the following encapsulation of my personal migrant experience may be of interest to many readers.

Before I start with the events, that developed out of our migration to Australia, I want to point out that there is not much in the way of good information about Australia and still less about its migration, both experientially and socioeconomically. A reason behind this might be that most migrants never reach the point of objectively documenting their experiences. In terms of migration, we are dealing with a silent majority of people who are otherwise thoroughly occupied with a battle to establish oneself in this new country of Australia. Thus, in writing this book, I acknowledge every individual migrant who has had to find his/her own way, to settle in an Australian multicultural society. There is neither valid rule detailing how to get there, nor pre-planned path to follow that should lead to a success. Rather more appropriate and timely is that every individual is asked to bring out his best, stay on that track and eventually success will ensue.

One has also to be flexible towards a new understanding of performance in a new environment; it is often at that point that problems often begin for a migrant. Keeping all this in mind, perhaps coupled with my individual experiences may prove to facilitate understanding.

Preface

- -

A Migration Process

Our plane took off from Kuala Lumpur in the middle of the night. As we gained height, the horizon in front of us announced first in dark red lines the new day, where Australia our future home was. With daylight, we passed its northwest from high up in the air. The ocean underneath, its coastlines, the land, all were inundated with incredible clear sunlight. Everything was clearly visible through the windows of our plane, but no houses, no roads.

Another five hours flight time to Melbourne in the far southeast gave a first impression of the size of this continent.

The main features one could see out of the plane were the vibrant colours of this land—dark red soil, dark to light green spots of vegetation, yellow–brown spots everywhere. Riverbeds were carved into this landscape, many do not carry water all year, they look like wild roads in a place that surpasses the horizon. Once the plane left the ocean behind, the blue colour of the water was almost missing, instead, green borders marked the course of a river.

Start in Frankfurt

Later on, roads became visible, straight thin lines right to the horizon. After four from a total of twenty-two hours of flight time over Australia, which started in the centre of Europe, we were over Adelaide, which was surrounded by hills. This was the first larger city in Australia that became visible in our flight path.

I happened to have a conversation with a gentleman from Monash University in Melbourne, who had briefed me in a very interesting way about this country of Australia. I have to admit, I have been in many countries around the world, but this was the first time I was on my way to Australia. Australia is not another country; Australia is a world of its own. The main reasons for this are: the distance to other parts of the world creates a natural isolation, the geological age of which is unmatched.

I still like to remember parts of discussions with the gentleman, when he pointed out that Australia's natural scales apply also to its people, in terms of the further north you go, the less formal people become. I promised to find out about it myself.

Now before setting foot in this country of our destination, we had to get ready to face new challenges. A good way to get prepared for such challenges was also to refresh our memory regarding what we knew about Australia. This was best done with a sense of humour, because who knew how our life really would develop?

Australia is located in the southern hemisphere; consequently, the seasons of the year are the opposite of the northern hemisphere, where we had come from. Summer in Europe means winter in Australia; summer in Australia again means winter in Europe. The sun shines in Australia from the north. In the south of this continent, it is cooler; in the north it is hotter throughout the year.

The crescent of the moon is hanging in the sky with its inner bow up. The coastline of Australia covers a total of 20 000 km. Perth in the west to Brisbane in the east makes 5 000 km, whilst Melbourne in the south to Darwin in the north makes approximately 4 000 km.

People generally know about the connection of Australia with England, but people not coming from 'Pom-land' are often surprised when they hear, Australia was still a 'colony' of England.

Australia seems to be too busy to comply with Commonwealth's good behaviour rules, such that they even overlooked the Queen's offer to be free to choose their own way. Australia is a very conservative society, they won't move from their present position in a hurry. In other words, there is a measure of good conservative 'colony' of England. This is a fact that a migrant has to be aware of. There is not much room for changes. It is advisable to embark on an 'underdog-role' as a new migrant in Australia.

Who are the Australians today? According to them, they are comprised of over seventy nations and they all call themselves 'Aussies'. They are also convinced that they are the 'lucky country', apparently based on an incredible natural wealth; the climate also spoiled its fifteen million citizens in 1981.

Australia is also a very harsh country, its own people reflect this through a controversy: you will find people who will give away their own shirt, to help the one in real need, there are others who are very efficient in making their fortune, do not get in their way!

We were about to land in Melbourne, 11 am local time, but not before a hiccough. Strong winds through patchy clouds made our plane skid off the runway, after the pilot dropped the plane apparently from too great a height; this demonstrated to us that not everybody was familiar with Australian conditions. We made it though, not without a real scare, after which the plane was actually taken out of service.

Before I announce the numbers and the make-up of the migrant party that set foot in Melbourne that day, I should like to let the reader know that this undertaking is put on paper over twenty-five years later.

Chapter 1

Start of a Migrant Life

I come now to the make-up of our party, which arrived in Melbourne in August 1981. We all arrived on that day—myself, my wife Arja, two boys and two girls. There was not enough time to take notice of the current weather conditions on our arrival, it was more important to us to follow the migration process on Australian soil.

We had no special expectations; the immigration procedures back in Germany were correct, I considered myself privileged. It certainly took quite a while to become accepted for migration. It appears that when the correct channels in a migration process are used, the response from the official Australian side is correct as well.

At the age of forty, I was on the age-limit for a migration, but this did not affect our plea for migration to Australia, because the average age of our family became considerably lower with our four children, aged between seven and twelve. Australia appeared to welcome families with children. Profound technical experience with sound English communication skills were other vital scoring points in the selection process. It would not have been wise to consider migration with all its implications when in possession of a questionable health status. Health is a vital condition for any success in a migration.

Our arrival in Australia unfolded as was indicated to us by the Australian Embassy in Germany: our luggage arrived with us and the controls were straightforward because we presented a list of contents. A small bus took us onboard with some other new arrivals, heading towards our first accommodation in a wide, established housing estate of the Australian Immigration Authorities—Midway Centre.

Melbourne—Midway Centre

The housing facility we became associated with had all the basic necessities to assist us in the planning of our new life in Australia. It was a great help to our family that basic meals were served in a centralised canteen. We also met two families during our first days in Australia, who had arrived with the same plane.

Despite the supportive facilities of our migration campus, we decided to start our new life in Australia as soon as possible.

I had a contact address of a machine-tool manufacturer in Melbourne. The owner was in his late seventies, and had arrived in the country twenty years earlier, not far from where we came. I made arrangements to meet with him at his firm, however at that meeting, he could not convince me to start with him. I perceived him to be a typical single performer, who unfortunately failed to appoint a supporting team in time to deal successfully with the complexities of such a business. (Incidentally, it took only two years for this modern company to disappear.) As this initial contact did not work out for me, I decided to look elsewhere, not necessarily in the immediate vicinity.

I can speak only on behalf of my family that the immigration processes were in accordance with the information given to us back in Germany, giving us no reason to complain. Such clear direction is undoubtedly the result of a government policy that had progressed into reality without noticeable discrepancies.

Now came the step into Australian daily life and it remained to be seen whether life in Australia would be also in accordance with migration efforts by the government.

The cold windy weather at our arrival in Melbourne made us look further north and find out about working and living conditions there. With the help of the migration authorities, I could leave my family in the hostel for a few days. I boarded a plane to Brisbane, the capital of Queensland, in northeast Australia in order to find out about that part of Australia.

Melbourne impressed us with its size and facilities, besides its unpredictable weather. The heads of the two families who had arrived with us in Melbourne, joined me in this excursion. One party could hardly speak English, the other one just managed. I could not help but ask myself, *how can somebody make such a decisive step of a migration with so little knowledge of the language?* Anyway, I did not mind helping out. Our trip to Brisbane was not covered by migration anymore, from now on, we had to run our own lives.

After a stopover in sunny Sydney, our plane arrived another good hour later further north in Brisbane. Everybody had to walk from the plane to the terminal of the airport; this was in early September 1981. The sun hit us out of a clear sky, the welcome to the Sunshine State no better introduction.

On our joint mission to Brisbane, we became also aware of its beautiful settings surrounded by nature. The city expanded into an ocean of single houses along a winding large river, only the green mountain range to the west limited this expansion. Tropical gardens surrounded each house, I thought that people must like their gardens here; even along streets many tropical trees had found their places.

Many houses were built in a typical Queensland style. They were raised off the ground with stumps, to give access to the air movement during summer, when it becomes very hot and humid. A veranda right around the house, under the same roof, latticework facing outside—everything was designed to protect from the intense sun.

Two high-rise buildings only soared to the city sky at that time. One of them was Parliament Building, which disappeared virtually in the skyscraper skyline of Brisbane twenty-five years later. Outstanding were: City Hall and Parliament building—a tiny stone church next to the other high rise buildings.

Our program to find work here began in the city; the yellow phone book with its business addresses became my starting point. I could secure in a short time two addresses with appointments. For technical reasons, I had to leave my two colleagues behind, while I tried the public transport system to get to appointment number one.

On my arrival, I rang the company from the railway station, as instructed. After only a short waiting time, a lady in a car stopped next to me asking, 'Are you Martin? ' I confirmed as much and joined her in the car. The few minutes drive to the company led through typical new industrial settings of mainly small companies, away from estates where people lived. A clean brick-building front surrounded a garden inviting the visitor into the office of a company. Company activity it seemed was established in tin sheds, which disappeared behind a facade. The whole terrain was carefully fenced, allowing passage only through a wide gate. The company I visited also fitted this image. Along with the owner I looked at a plastic-injection- moulding area with its own tool room facility, the impression was not overwhelming, although I could not deny the owner's vitality and his sense of pride in this setup.

I recall thinking to myself, I am in a new country; any comparison with another country would be fruitless. I decided to 'take the plunge' and accepted the employment offer. This way, my immediate problem was solved; this already on the first day. Things started to look bright for us.

Back in the city of Brisbane, all three of us found a place to sleep for the night at the Peoples Palace, directly next to Central Station, in the heart of the city. My room was high up in this corner building.

We decided to have an early rest after a long busy day. Looking out through my window into a sea of lights, I was surprised at how clear the atmosphere of this city appeared. A part of the starry southern-sky shone clear over this city, where the buildings left space. The activities, the noise from the streets vanished during the night, enabling everyone to then have a good night's sleep in Peoples Palace of Brisbane.

The next day, we decided to find work in a joint effort for one colleague of this excursion. The other one showed no interest in finding work.

A fundamental fact of migration started to emerge: it became evident with time that migrants who were insufficiently prepared for migration were less likely to succeed in their goals. Moreover, a background of considerable finance is not necessarily a warrant for success; the task remains to secure this start and build on it. It appeared that, the less somebody carries with him, the better his or her chances to integrate into a new environment.

Let me analyse the circumstances that are surrounding a person who seeks and finally practices migration. I'd like to answer here two main questions out of my own experiences: why do people migrate ? Who are the people that undertake migration?

There is a legal and illegal migration. No reliable figures are on hand to indicate which kind of migration is dominant throughout the world, although having said that, the reality would indicate that a high percentage of illegal migration is taking place. I believe that there is a scenario in place whereby some people force their issues onto people of another society in order to gain access to a better future. This I believe to be the driving force behind illegal migration. The fact remains that there are still more poor people in this world, perhaps courtesy of illegal migration.

Within the general public, not much is known about illegal migration. Most of the time we become aware of such activities only on the doorsteps of our countries, or more recently, in our own backyard.

In Brazil migration is happening within its own borders. The south with its industry has drawn people in their millions from the underdeveloped north. A result of the illusion of a better life in the south can be seen in the formation of the 'favellas' (slums), where failed migration concentrates in the middle of pulsing wealth. This uncontrolled migration rapidly morphs into social problems for everybody.

America has a traditional problem as well with illegal migration from its south, mainly from Mexico. In the past, the liberal society of the United States has found a way to offer illegal people for lower conditions work. Lately, this has developed into a situation, whereby the American people were forced to admit that the country would cease to run without this illegal workforce.

I encountered an individual case on a business trip to Germany in 1987, which is worthy of mention, because it underpins the reality under which illegal migration happens around us. During my stay in Germany, I frequently used the public train system to get around. On one occasion, a man took the seat opposite me, when the train left the city of Hannover. This new passenger was dressed in a suit and carried no luggage with him.

His deep black hair and dark skin indicated an origin from the Indian Sub-Continent. The gentleman tried to introduce himself in a few German words, which I could not understand. His accent told me immediately that he certainly was more familiar with English. So I returned his introduction in English. His expression was that of sur- prise. Now he began to converse with me in English, his words came out like a cascade: 'How can I find work in Germany? ' he asked me.

I inquired as to how he had arrived in Germany, and learned that he was from Pakistan. He was obviously delighted to talk to somebody about his problems. He also confessed openly to me that he arrived in East Berlin; entering West Germany only a few years before the unification. The East-German Regime freely pushed off its uneasy visitors to West Germany. I made my co-passenger aware that he would face problems in terms of finding work. Moreover, considering the way he entered Germany, he was better advised to return to his country and seek work through legal channels.

This was not what he wanted to hear, so he moved on within the train, looking for somebody else to help his case.

I wondered how many others pushed their luck through illegal migration? In most cases, only a migrant knows the outcome of such a move for a 'better life'. Hope that illegal cases of a migration do not turn into a form of crime, in which they can find themselves out of desperation always remains as a last resort.

Societies are like 'walls' in the way of migration movements. With time, only small numbers of illegal cases manage to obtain better conditions for themselves. Most of the time, illegal migration is bound to fail in its process; a new kind of hardship takes over. This is one of the fundamental differences between legal and illegal migration; legal migration has still a better chance to succeed.

To answer my case, I refer to Heinrich Heine, a German writer, who said in his exile in England, 'I think of Germany at night, I lose my sleep.' Otherwise, there are a number of issues, that lead to a decision of a migration: adventure, trying to 'run away from something', determination to find better living conditions, or to work out better living conditions, sometimes even a naivety towards new conditions, fortune hunter, flight of capital; very rarely to escape a lawsuit, that slipped past the attention of a thorough process, which Australia is maintaining.

It would be unfair to use a picture of the past, when convicts were deported to Australia. Most cases were poverty-stricken subjects and very often uneasy persons within the society of that time. There is no reliable number of real 'crooks', who were forced to migrate to Australia.

However, generally speaking, somebody reaching out for migration, moving towards considerable changes, has to be a person who is different from current mainstream.

It also cannot be denied that every individual who migrates, carries a 'package' with him, that can unfold successfully, or lead to failure. No matter what such package holds, at the end, the outcome of a migration move is determined by the capacity of an individual to adjust to new conditions.

Now coming briefly to the 'recruits' of a migration process or, who is migrating: definitely people of all levels of a society—the poor are driven by a desire for a better life, most of the time, they are lacking of the means to support a process towards a migration; professional qualified middle class is the more desirable and more successful group for migration, representing the mainstream in legal migration.

Allowing refugees without means to migrate is a measure to help ease misery in this world; such a move can be seen also as 'educated guilt' towards the world around us.

In later years in Australia, I experienced three particular migration cases during my function as a Technical Manager. Three young men from South East Asia managed in separate incidents to arrive in Australia under extreme conditions by boat; known in Australia as boat people. After some time, they began work at our company as labourers, showing a strong will to work hard. From time to time, the company recruited people for further in house training from this workforce, who had excelled in all aspects of their work. Three boat people qualified one after the other for this selection. Despite a certain lack of knowledge in English, all three reached qualifications in a trade with excellence.

Prior to my Australian experience, I learnt that best results can oftentimes be developed from 'disadvantaged' people of a society, not necessarily the poorest. My three boat people also showed continuous strong interest; they were very fast learners, always disciplined, highly adaptable. No surprise that many years later, all three began independently their own successful, high-tech businesses.

To give people a chance in their life and see them through for many years, is highly rewarding.

I return to my second day in Brisbane—a colleague of ours needed work; (whereas another colleague, also from our 'expedition', was reluctant to seek work, opting instead to rely on the fortune that he had brought with him to Australia) These two colleagues out of Germany presented a vastly different scenario to that of the three boat-people as previously discussed.

Poverty does not mean less intelligence; rather, it is the opposite in my opinion. To endure poverty asks for more strength than does living in prosperity, which is in general afforded through a system.

An interview was consequently arranged for the first colleague, during which I helped out with most of the talking. I observed during the interview an approach, which emerged on this occasion: the other party, the employer, asked very basic questions. At a first glance, this appeared to be an easy entrance into this job. However, I could not prevent our colleague of emerging at the end of this conversation with the words: 'I can do this with my left hand'. At first I thought we had lost our case with such an expression, however, the employer lent a helping hand and with a smile, a starting date was offered in return.

Our task accomplished in Brisbane, we cut short our time; from now on, it was up to everybody of our trio to get his own life started in Australia. I took the next flight back to Melbourne to arrange for my family to undertake the move to Brisbane.

What was colleague number one thinking when he produced *that* statement? Sure, in Germany, colleague number one was a respected professional person, according to him. This respect gave colleague number one a remarkable sense of self-confidence at such remark- ably inappropriate timing. Outside this traditional understanding in Germany, there was a new focus on life situations required in Australia; like stepping back, observing, learning to play as a migrant the appropriate 'underdog' role.

With time, someone eventually listens to the migrant voice. A new country like Australia is run a specific way; a few migrants won't change this course. Incidentally, I'd like to mention beforehand that colleague number one remained only a very short period of time in the position he had been offered. He resigned shortly afterwards, producing all kind of accusations directed at his employment situation. He apparently continued to have problems of the same nature, and abandoned his professional confidence in Australia once for all. At least he continued working, distributing goods around town. Number two colleague embarked on a smarter course and sat back on an early pension.

During the course of this written undertaking, I return to focus on a fact that even on the legal migration side there is a significantly high percentage of migrants that fail in their migration aspirations.

There is a proverb from the past, referring to migration, 'The first deals with death, the second (generation) with misery, the third will have bread.' Things have changed since, but elements of hardship remain in place.

The reason I point out certain experiences here with a documentation of facts is that there is very little material written by migrants themselves. One reason for this could be that a long lasting struggle to get somewhere in a country prevents migrants reflecting objectively on their life—objectivity is lost in the endless struggle. There is undoubtedly much suppressed understanding in migrants, which impacts negatively. In particular with those people who expected to have problems from their native country abolished when they arrived in a new country. The way a migrant adapts to a new situation helps him to leave behind perceived problems; integration into a new and different society can be facilitated. There is never a guarantee that one's problems in a new country will be less.

There is certainly the strong, determined migrant character, but there is also the less strong and less determined migrant. This variation in personalities is to a high degree responsible for the outcome of a migration. Every individual has to find his own way to succeed; there is no recipe to pass on successfully from one to another.

Why migration, when this is anything but the easy path? Migration is a fundamental challenge; he who masters the steps towards success, accepts, in a broad sense, to work more than he ever thought of; thus this migrant has managed to change into a new environment and therefore, the range of possibilities becomes much wider for this individual.

During my life, I have heard expressions like: 'I also could have achieved something in my native country, if I had worked so hard.' This is the voice of a migrant, who made it—he acknowledged the efforts he had to make to succeed. The difference from his native country however lies in the nature of his achievements.

Migration can be seen as a process of being 'stripped of one's feathers', before a process of rebuilding can begin. How an individual manages to get through such unknown pre-conditions attached to migration depends on the character formation of an individual. Every outcome in migration is unpredictable. At the end of success, what becomes visible is money, but not so visible is the origin of this money. Success or failure through migration remains most of the time a hidden story. Is that why, realistically, so little is expressed by migrants?

The complexity of life through migration in part explains the diversity of migration outcomes.

Back to Melbourne, where we arrived after two days in Brisbane. From now on each member of this Brisbane excursion had to run its own affairs. Before I took off with my family, we experienced an occurrence that oftentimes is somewhat typical of the migrant experience—money we had paid into a bank account wasn't available to us anymore, due to conditions attached to the account having been missed or overlooked. Moreover, one colleague of mine received his account book back bearing a completely different name. Had this discrepancy not been discovered, our colleague from Germany would conceivably have lost all his money. There is good reason for the immigration authorities in Australia advocating caution to be exercised with money on arrival; purchases of land, housing, car, in particular.

The weather was fine as we left Melbourne in a brand new Qantas Airlines Airbus. Qantas stands for 'Queensland and Northern Territory Air Services', is not only one of the largest airline organisations, along with KLM, it is also one of the oldest airlines in the world. Long before other well-known airlines took off, Qantas was servicing Queensland and the Northern Territory. At that beginning, these flights were real adventures. Experiences were made, that over an eighty year period, helped Qantas to emerge as a very successful and very safe airline. Qantas can be regarded as one of the successful enterprises of this country; their discipline reflects work life in Australia.

At the time of our arrival, Qantas was, with perfection and profit, servicing other airlines from around the world in Australia. This must have changed in over two decades in Australia, as at one point, Qantas intended to shift their maintenance services overseas, because of high costs in Australia. Who wants to put a price on safety here ? The Australian public responded unanimously, opting to pay more, if obliged, to retain the services of Qantas in the country.

On our arrival in Brisbane, 'Capital of the Sunshine State', a classic sunny day welcomed us. As we were a few days prior still in a relatively low-sunlight environment of Middle Europe, we were now stunned by the brightness of the sun during the day in Queensland and our children began to complain of headaches.

When our plane landed this time with all six of us in Brisbane, we had to walk our way to the terminal again. This first encounter with Brisbane gave the impression of a stylish country town with no rush for progress in mind. In the years to come, it became evident that we had arrived before Brisbane started to develop into the fastest growing capital of the continent.

Brisbane, Queensland—Wacol Migrant Hostel—September 1981

As I experienced, the weather is a dominant issue in Australia; it is discussed daily—its people displaying a readiness to assist others in the community at times of hardship resulting from weather anomalies. The climate shapes and forms people to a large degree; extreme weather conditions appear to bring out very helpful, friendly people. The brilliant sunny days of September must have been around for quite a number of weeks, if not months—the yellow/brown grass indicating this. The locals stating that 'rain comes with the wet season and it's just around the corner'.

We headed from the airport to Wacol, south of Brisbane, to the migration hostel. In Melbourne, migration had organised a temporary transfer to a hostel in Brisbane for us. I could provide employment evidence for them. (I realise only now, that the Wacol hostel was very close to my workplace, which was fortunate for me.)

We did not expect luxury in the Wacol hostel. Between scattered eucalypt trees were a number of barracks-like accommodations, built out of timber and raised from the ground in the tradition of Queensland style houses.

Two rooms with their own entrances were given to us. The beds were covered with heavy wool blankets. After sunset, we learnt why we were supplied with such blankets—the beginning of September was still wintertime there. As soon as the brilliant warm sun disappeared during the day, cold air moved in with the night. In a separate building, we were offered basic meals which gave us the time to start organising our new life better. After such eventful days, a good night's sleep became a necessity.

Another day started with bright sunlight rising slowly over the horizon, consuming the cold of the night and returning a warm sunny day.

The weather is full of contrasts on this continent: the south is rather wet in winter, whereas the north is dry during winter, stretching from June to September. Again, the opposite occurs during summer from October until April where the south becomes usually dry; the north is dealing with a wet and hot season.

Environmental changes do not stop at Australia's doorstep; they are also becoming evident elsewhere. It remains to be seen, how long such a stable weather pattern, as I described, will remain in place. We still know too little about weather changes of the past, to forecast changes to come.

Our main concern remained to get our new life started here. Besides our family, hardly any other newcomers were in this hostel.

One young couple from Switzerland claimed that for a period of a year, they could not find any rental accommodation. On top of that, they were very negative about their new life in Australia. We decided to ignore such contribution; people talk a lot and experience has shown that what is relevant for one, is far from binding for somebody else.

We moved on immediately. A brief visit to the nearby company had the result that I could start any day.

It was sensible to organise beforehand a couple of things, like the Australian driver's license for their left-side traffic; this was then a formality at a police station, where I had to answer in writing a number of questions, to prove that I understood English sufficiently.

Another important question emerged: where can we live ? Before sunset, the question was answered: In Inala, outside its centre, in a quiet street, we signed a contract to rent a complete house with a nice established garden.

The rent was within reason, particularly when I think back to what rental situations were like where we came from. The blooming frangipani in front of the stairs, which led into the house, ranking palms and a big round and dense mango tree in the back yard, provided a welcome that could not have been better for us.

Brisbane—Inala

For a number of years we hesitated to buy a property in Germany, because we experienced more desirable accommodations in other parts of the world during the course of our family life. We made our decision for Australia, when we lived and worked in South Africa and Brazil. Our children missed the natural colours of these environments—sun, blue skies, palms, colourful birds, flowers, wild life, distances. Here in Australia we got most of this back, life had to be easier this way? Of course, I had had to run around from real estate to real estate, calling private phone numbers out of the newspaper, talking to people directly, but in the end we found something, a place from where we could start. Until this stage of our arrival in Australia, we moved into a direction that is promoted by the official migration department of this country. From now on it remained to be seen how our arrival integrated with the people and their views. Government initiatives are not always backed up by a majority of the population. Politicians are like children in the sandpit, they throw occasionally sand towards each other, which does not help their vision.

Australia has still one plus for its migration plans—new migrants can move within its huge territory; boundaries in their broadest sense do not yet interfere in an individual's life like in densely populated parts of the world. Australia can still offer everybody the chance to escape into something or somewhere else. This is also a basis for the construction of Australia's multicultural society. It also remains to be seen in Australia, how a future will respond to its shrinking boundaries and opportunities, through a denser population.

Chapter 2

Efforts to Settle

Our self-constructed container with all our household goods must have been at sea, somewhere between Europe and Australia. Until its arrival, we had to find ways to overcome shortages in all sort of things. As soon as I commenced regular work, colleagues helped freely to accommodate us in our empty house. We were really moved by such prompt and unconditional help. We responded with a barbecue and the all-important beer; our empty house did not matter, the occasion took place outside under the shade of the big mango tree with the barbecue installations next to it. We all had every reason to feel at home.

Our four children paid the nearest school a visit. The language did not present a problem; children find ways to communicate. The teachers were very helpful with the integration of our children into school. Each child started at the appropriate level, for a few days simply observing class activities, they participated in the lessons soon after.

Our children started at a public school rather than at a private school, because we thought it would provide a more realistic integration into the local community. When our children came home with their new school friends, it became very obvious that these friends did not pay much attention to our house not being furnished as yet. This contact became very friendly and open, even if there had been some curiosity in the initial stages.

At work, I began to notice and think about differences between my present and previous work experiences. Everybody was here everybody's 'mate', and I believed it was a good praxis to follow this 'rule' to gain acceptance in a mainly male working environment. On one occasion a colleague, originally from Bavaria in Germany and with a very dominant character, told me that, 'The Australians are like savages.'. I simply listened to those words without adding any comments; I would have been crazy to judge people after only a few weeks in the country.

When I write this twenty-five years later, I would respond in this manner: 'Savages' base their judgement of others on very straight- forward instincts. One instinct relates to performance—Australia asks for performance, its people are keen to cheer a performer, but condemn just as quickly when the performer loses.

In later years, I heard from discussions with Chinese businessmen: 'Somebody who makes it in Australia, will make it anywhere in the world'. Let us wait and see during the course of this written exercise, how our migrant family could hold their ground.

Coming back to work, I tried my best to get over the first hurdles. One of them consisted of a mixture in the imperial and metric systems. Officially, Australia had adopted the metric system, but the old habit with imperial fractions of measurements lived on in a parallel way. For us, the trick to avoiding confusion within those two systems lay in safeguarding only one system at a time and not translating from one into the other.

A working day in Brisbane had official breaks like in Germany. The difference is that a food-van arrived there on the roadside near company premises, where most of the staff could purchase junk food like hot dogs, hamburgers and a coke. I chose to bring my lunch from home, the main reason being to keep a close eye on the economical side of life in our family.

Mostly sunny weather invited one to have a break outdoors. Eat- ing lunch in the hot sun was however in my view not a great idea. I opted to stay indoors for that reason, particularly after some trials in the company of my workmates. Lunch in the Australian sun means cooking the lot again, including oneself.

Many Australian men consider themselves tough; therefore, some elected to ignore conditions that may lead to a number of skin-cancer related health problems. We are living here in the skin-cancer-capital of the world, protection against the sun here is widely recommended. The only effective protection being to stay out of the sun!

Anyway, work continued in Australia. I was not sure from the start about my role in this workplace. I had the task of programming machine tools with two other mates, resulting in a scenario whereby when their efforts worked out good, this counted on their books; problems were shifted onto my account. The two mates successfully kept me out of their territory; I could not help but feel like a fifth wheel. Was this something a migrant *had to* endure ?

At the end of September, when the temperature along with the humidity rose by the day, the first storm arrived after a long dry winter. I have experienced storms in other parts of the world, but nothing like this.

For a little under an hour, high winds dumped so much water out of a blue–black sky that everything in its path submerged, the water could not f low away quickly enough. I was still at work when the water rushed through all of the buildings, cutting power; instantly everybody had to take refuge on a higher spot like a chair or table and work ceased altogether. Our boss could not even use his own power generator—a huge diesel engine, which was connected from the outside to the factory—as it was not safe anymore to operate due to the water in the building. (This backup power supply was a precautionary measure in order to stay operational during the frequent power cuts; indeed in those years, aerial power lines in themselves proved to be a recipe for power failure in the event of a storm.) The lightning and the rumble of the thunder disappeared to the north; it did not take long for the late afternoon sun to re-establish its regime. As a result of this storm though, all major roads became flooded. I did not arrive home until the middle of the night, where everything was fine. The house on its stumps had remained out of reach of the torrents.

Sudden floods are a constant problem in Australia, if not a danger. Leichhardt, an early explorer from Germany, disappeared in North Queensland together with his team, nobody knows where and how. It is assumed that they were most likely caught by flash floods, which often originate far away. This is demonstrated by the fact that even in bright sunshine, a sudden wall of water can hit those in low-lying areas. Australia is also the continent where most rivers carry little or no water in dry riverbeds called creeks, which can rapidly become raging torrents.

Additionally, in terms of rainfall, I found one main difference between Australia and other countries. For instance, in comparison with climates of Brazil, here, after a storm the temperature drops considerably and makes life comfortable again, whereas in Brazil it remains hot and humid. (A couple of years after that first storm, I worked with a company that manufactured building products and I noticed in their engineering department that rain gutters for houses were calculated for a downfall of 250 mm per hour. This caters for a lot of water, considering that during an entire year in Germany, rainfall is around only 400 to 500 mm.)

The next day, the sun absorbed all this humidity and made the day rather uncomfortable again. Another storm also arrived the following day, exactly at the same time in the afternoon. I asked myself, how is it that Australia is considered the driest country on earth? Summer 1981/1982, October until April, represented the start of a number of exceptionally wet and hot seasons in Queensland, which made for a rather difficult situation for us, who were attempting to settle and become accustomed to our new country.

My wife also carried another future member of our family, who joined us early 1982. We were determined to put up with these new conditions in Australia, rather than to accept the conditions where we came from.

Our container eventually arrived from overseas and I had to unload all its contents directly from a truck, because the driver had no lifting facility to accommodate the weight of the container. It was hot, humid and wet on that day, the air completely still. What a job! A challenge lay ahead for all of us, for only when the empty container was dropped from the truck, the job was over. To keep cool during unloading, countless buckets of water went over our heads.

The days could not be long enough to rearrange our household from overseas though. Time rushed towards the end of 1981. The hot and wet summer decided to stay with us.

First self-made furniture (solid New Guinea teak)

At work, I had begun to ask myself what kind of a future was avail- able to me. There was no answer in sight. My mates loved modern music, which was broadcast all day long from a local radio station. This was something new for me and something I hadn't experienced before—an easy-going way of life. The majority of the staff weren't distracted in any way, they rather enjoyed themselves and felt relaxed. It also depended somewhat on what kind of work was being undertaken as to whether or not distraction occurred. This raised a few issues for me—is it that the ample space in Australia facilitates the expression of noise to travel more freely, than say in many other parts of the world? And, if so, are Aussies less stressed than their European counterparts because of this?

The time that was left me after a day's work, I utilised in building at home some proper furniture instead of buying it. Our home was big enough to claim one room only for this activity. At that time, Australia still had available timbers from Malaysia, Indonesia and Papua New Guinea. Compared with Europe, the price of tropical hard woods was very low in Australia. During the weeks before Christmas, I created some outstanding furniture.

In the middle of the night, when I still worked on this furniture, a good friend from my hometown in Germany turned up at our doorsteps without notice. This friend had combined pleasure with work on a tour to Australia, by advising prospective investors in a sugarcane enterprise in Bundaberg, north of Brisbane. Not a bad selection I must say! Thus doing, he could experience a phase of development in the life of a migrant.

Christmas time is a very different event in the southern hemisphere as opposed to Christmas in Europe. In the middle of the summer with its fierce heat, a carnival atmosphere prevails. There is not much of a peaceful time, what with everything in the nature around us exploding into new growth. An abundance of colour is created, people enjoying this display in many ways. When in Australia, not everyone continues the tradition of Christmas with a fir tree, perhaps because there is more than enough light during Australia's Christmastime or maybe because fir trees are not grown in Australia.

Some people attend religious services on Christmas Eve, which has a vague origin in English tradition, I believe. Christmas day passes around a party, at home with family, very often outside the house around a swimming pool. Contrary to most parts of Europe, including England, there is no Christmas 'Peace' in Australia, pubs stay open.

The population in Australia consists of many nationalities, thus, not everybody celebrates Christmas, but the ones that do also exchange presents. In Germany, this takes place on Christmas Eve under a bright Christmas tree. In Australia, presents are given on Christmas Day morning, when the family gets out of bed. This custom is similar to the tradition of Nicholaus—Santa Claus in Germany.

Most businesses are closed between Christmas and New Year. People usually take holidays and the whole nation is on the move. Popular sandy beaches are then crowded with swimmers, sun-seekers, surfers and sport-players. The 20 000 kilometres of coastline leaves plenty of room for an escape, although attention has also to be paid to regulations on beaches. Those regulations are observed on many popular beaches by voluntary lifesavers. Further north, the ocean becomes increasingly dangerous with its sea life, such that swimming is no longer allowed. Yet, each summer the ocean claims the lives of incautious people.

Our first Christmas in Australia was not quite a new experience for us as we had already celebrated two Christmas in Brazil. We took the opportunity to arrange Christmas the way we used to celebrate home in Germany. In Australia, every individual has the freedom to relate to their own customs, without fear of recrimination. Thus, there are many and diverse traditions being observed across the nation. This might be also the reason that, with the exception of some places in South Australia, the rest of the continent does not experience church-bell ringing, as is the case in parts of Europe (at Christmas—every day!). The multitude of customs in Australia has an added benefit in that it does not allow for one particular custom to dominate another. With respect to other countries, everybody has to practice tolerance, by allowing other customs to live in harmony together, without the taint of single mindedness.

Our tree on Christmas Eve was a pine, a close copy of a fir tree in Germany. Its lights were electrical; real candles would have been too hot and too much of a fire hazard. The decorations were a collection of items, which were inherited within our families, going back to Transylvania and Finland; some later items were presents or self-made. Once the bell rang, the door opened to the room with the Christmas tree. Together, we sang some common Christmas carols followed by a recorder and a guitar.

We all wore festive summer clothes, no suit or costume. The musical part was followed by the gift presentation: one child at the time picked a gift from under the tree, looked at the label and passed it on to that person with personal Christmas wishes. It did not take long for everybody to be surrounded by wrapping papers. A little assistance from all sides helped to separate the gifts from the piles of gift papers.

In order to keep our relationships alive, we spoke to our families overseas on the telephone; everybody in the family taking a turn.

Dinner followed in another room, not so much in a traditional way, but with the focus more on current temperature conditions; we preferred not to eat too rich or too heavy. The festivity became a family event.

In later years, we had also selected friends with us. Our Christmas ended usually late in the night, after the children had familiarised themselves with their presents.

There was no rush in the morning of the following day, though in the early hours of that morning, we went out to the fantastic nature of southeast Queensland, we had a better chance of missing Christmas traffic congestion if we left early.

Sunshine Coast Queensland—north of Brisbane

During our first Christmas, we also paid a visit to the nearest beach. A constant cool breeze makes life on a beach quite comfortable for most of the time. Further inland, this cooling effect from the ocean disappears and as a consequence, temperatures soar. The beach invited everybody to relax—with its fine white sands, blue–green ocean waters with white caps on top of their waves, clear sunny skies under a clean atmosphere, it was ideal to allow that to soak deep into our lungs. All these natural elements seemed the perfect setting for walking, swimming in proximity of the sandy beach, riding the waves, resting, playing, digging in the sand, talking, sharing a drink with some light food and giving our fantasy a new course. As time progressed during the day, more people turned up, a beach society developed, everybody let each other live the way they wanted. It never became really crowded, everybody had enough space for their own activities. We enjoyed this life very much, because we had lived most of the time far away from an ocean.

The unique location of Brisbane offers within close distance not only beaches, but also mountain ranges and dense rainforests. Further west the Australian bush begins, as do grasslands in between the ranges of the Great Divide, all before the endless Outback. Civilisation eventually stopped here at the doorsteps of a city, where the Australian nature took over.

Christmas break was a short one for me, because I had not many leave days during the few months since our start in Australia. The weather continued with regular storms through that summer, after a daily peak in extreme temperature.

Life back at work again looked quite different from the Christmas break days, the heat during the day made work extremely demanding.

We Europeans came to Australia with our own work ethics and had forgotten that we now lived in a different part of the world. To find a way to manage such new conditions and progress, is something that a migrant will inevitably face.

Coming to our case, I could not see in my first workplace any progress in that arena. At the end of January 1982, our first Aussie was born in the middle of a big thunderstorm, at a hospital where the conditions we met were of a high standard. Our daughter later became the music genius in the family. I started to look for other work shortly afterwards.

Chapter 3

- -

Moves in a New Life

In coming weeks I made contacts to Perth, in Western Australia. As I had a few addresses, I took a couple of days off from my current work, to take a plane to Perth, nearly 5 000 kilometres to the west. I had to go via Sydney to board a plane to Perth. After five hours in the air above this vast continent with its colourful carpet of nature, the sunshine welcomed me also in Perth, the capital of Western Australia. The f lies of Western Australia inspected me, the new arrival, with insistence. That's how you learn the Australian way of a welcome, when you wave with your hand continually in front of your face, to keep the f lies away. This is one distinct difference to Brisbane, where you don't have to do this.

Perth stretches along an Indian Ocean bay, to the east the land raises to the Darling Range. Rich mining activities in this huge territory offer opportunities for those who can make a prosperous living out of it. I spent one day mainly in one place, where I wanted to find out how this Italian entrepreneur worked and what his work was like in plastic injection moulding. At the end of this day, I decided not to join.

Before leaving Perth, I decided to have a closer look around. Very old trees in the middle of the city gave a respectable impression of the age of this part of Australia, next to modern buildings that soared to the sky in concrete and glass. A vast park surrounds Perth to its north-east; it holds a great variety of the unique flora and fauna, like the delicate colourful Kangaroo Paw, West Australia's national emblem. One could encounter with more time, on the shores of this city, the other natural emblem, the black swan, which exclusively calls Perth its home. All in all, I left Western Australia for the time being on a positive note—the climate was generally drier than the sub-tropical part of southeast Queensland.

Back in Queensland, I then found a note from a Perth business that expressed interest in my application. As I gained some knowledge of the place during my brief visit, the negotiations with this latest employment opportunity took place over a couple of phone calls. I asked for a written confirmation of the development in our discussions, which I received. A new hopeful direction was found for our life in Australia. The technical side, how to get us there, asked for systematic and decisive action.

So it was that at the end of April 1982 we were ready to move to a new destination in Western Australia. Our household goods went back into our container, on-call storage was organised. Unanimously the whole family agreed that we drive our car from Brisbane through New South Wales and South Australia, following the Nullarbor route to Western Australia. During this tour we learned first hand much more about Australia.

Northwest New South Wales (Tour to Perth)

On our tour, we were partly alone for hours. There was a tradition outside populated areas, to pass a greeting sign to a bypassing vehicle; this told both parties that everybody was doing fine. Help was not a question; it was a must, if one wanted to survive.

Water, tools, petrol and food had to be an essential company on a tour in Australia! We took our time as in South Australia kangaroos crossed the road in their hundreds. Many of them did not make it, mainly hit by big trucks.

The problem with kangaroos is their capability to jump suddenly out of the bush right in front of a car, hardly any time is then left for a driver to react. Our car was fitted with a bull-bar on its front, which can to certain degree protect from an impact with a kangaroo. There was other wildlife to watch as well, the wombat for instance is compact and low, an encounter with it can cause many problems. More commonly, farmers in the south of Australia have fence arrangements in place to keep their cattle on their property. Further north however, as I experienced, farms become so large, cattle are controlled from the air by a helicopter and on the ground by stockmen on horses. An unexpected encounter with cattle can have a fatal outcome for a car and the driver.

On our tour to Western Australia, we saw mountain passes, dense forest, vast open farming land, grasslands and Australian bush. Around Broken Hill, we noticed a slight desert impression, then lonely Flinders Mountain Ranges, wheat farming in Eyre Peninsula with its silo stations, Nullarbor Plain and the route along the Great Australian Bight. 'Nullarbor', because only bush can hide from the continuous strong winds that come from Antarctica.

A homestead on the side of this road reminded us how dangerous it was in the past to travel here. A family called Ross tried to settle there— they all perished because of a lack of drinking water. They would have found water very close to where they tried to settle, if they had communicated with the few Aborigines in the area. The South Australian Government is today maintaining this stone building of the Ross family, serving as a reminder for by-passers how difficult times were in the past.

Ross Family Home in the Nullarbor (South Australia)

Nullarbor petrol station office sign

On a small petrol station along this road, we observed a sign behind the window of the station, saying 'In God we trust, all others pay cash'; this was a nice way to express a cautious mentality of the few people that lived here.

On occasion, I like to highlight a memorable incident that happened at that time. At various times we could see from our car wedge-tailed eagles, huge birds of prey. I had a strong intention to get a photo of a wedge-tailed eagle. I was therefore on the lookout for this occasion. The occasion arrived and could not have been better. A big wedge-tailed eagle was sitting on a dead kangaroo, on the opposite side of the road. We hadn't seen any other car for hours on this road. At exactly that time, there had to be a big truck behind me, preventing me from taking my eagle photo. I will never forget this eye-to-eye contact with this huge eagle. The eagle looked towards me with staring eyes, an incredible experience. The eagle was not sure whether to stay on its prey or to move and must have known from experience that as long as a vehicle moves, he can remain in his position. I was robbed of my eagle photo when only two metres away from it; an occasion that will not be repeated.

We also passed the Great Australian Bight, a remarkable scene on its own. The road came close to its rocky steep walls just before we reached Eucla, the border town of Western Australia. From our elevated position, we could see deep down the white crests of waves from the Southern Ocean, how their power was broken here. As far as the eye could see, the rock walls limited the sea in a gradual bow. The sky above was blue like the sea, the sun broke the continuous stiff breeze, bush knuckled under in various greens.

Eucla is the formal border town of Western Australia; but there is of course no visible border. In the centre of this small town, a monument of a whale reminded one of the past activities of its people. Since Australia abandoned whale hunting, Eucla had had to find other business activities. Today the town counts more on tourists for its economy. A complex sign in its small centre indicates directions and distances to major cities in the world. This shows just how far this place is from anywhere.

Sign in the centre of Eucla

Hand sign: Everything is Okay

South Australian Bight (Cliff heights = 80 metres)

Historical wagon

Darling Ranges before Perth (Black-Boy or Grass Tree—approx 5000 years old)

The road changed suddenly in Caiguna. The previous straight road dropped significantly further down to the coast at that point, from then on, the road remained on that level for the most part. Elevations followed in parallel towards the inland; the formation of which could have something to do with a moraine out of ancient ice ages, possibly originating from the Antarctica.

Before our road turned from Norseman to the north, we travelled in the South of Western Australia through parts of forests that lined both sides of the road. Eucalypt trees stood tall behind a ditch, which directed water away from the road.

The weather was fine all the way being typical Australian weather and we didn't experience one drop of rain. In Coolgardie, the West Australian goldmine town, we could not see much activity; the place looked like a ghost town though suggestive of other, better times. We stopped in town to give the family a break from driving. The children found a place to dig for gold. They realised however, finding gold was not that easy, a slight disappointment on their faces became inevitable.

The time dictated our departure. Our destination of Perth came closer; within one day's trip. The flat open country to Perth is the wheat belt of Western Australia. To both sides of the road, the land was ploughed and prepared for the next crop, the only trees there lining the road.

Shortly before we reached Perth, this scenery changed, to be replaced by the dense bush and forest covering the Darling Ranges. Grass-trees in large clumps came in sight, their size telling the story of their age. Everything was transformed into a world of its own; rich, diverse, natural and unexpected.

Next to our road appeared a pipe system, which delivered water from this higher region down to Perth on the coast. The road followed that pipe system downhill. Perth received us in its western suburbs on the foothills, where we came from. On our arrival, we had clear sunny weather, the air felt dry and the temperature could be called rather mild, when compared with Queensland.

Our trip went without incident; everybody looked forward to this challenge in a new part of Australia.

A street directory of Perth became one of the first things we looked at to find the address of the company in Valencia. As the name of this suburb of Perth suggests, people from the southern parts of Europe lived there also, they have given their new residences names in commemoration of their native country. We found the address we were after in the northeast of Perth, on the boundary with the Australian bush. A high fence marked off the territory of the company from the surrounding bush land. The proud owner, a gentleman from Germany, spoke to us only in English.

As we arrived on a Saturday, the company was not operational, although, the company presented itself in an organised, very clean and modern way. I was pleased with what I saw; we hoped the rest would not be too far from this positive first impression.

Naturally, one of the first concerns was to find an answer regarding where we could stay. Temporary house accommodation gave us the much-needed rest over this first weekend. New conditions hold always surprises, which we experienced the next day, early on a Sunday morning. A real estate agent obviously did not know about our presence in this house, when the door opened and he started to show a number of clients the premises. He didn't progress very far in his undertaking, because he stood right in front of our provisional floor-beds, next to the entrance. This obvious embarrassment begged an explanation from both sides; the case became quickly settled.

Monday a week later, we were accommodated in a house, not far from the company. On this occasion, we became acquainted with the business partner of our German gentleman. Obviously the house had something to do with the business partner's interest. Nevertheless, not a bad start with a rented house for our own use, a fenced back yard and front garden facing the road.

Our new course of life was set in Western Australia. I commenced work immediately in the nearby company. My wife enrolled our children in school and they began their school lives in a new uniform. The wearing of school uniforms is not a bad arrangement in Australia; reflecting a common approach towards discipline.

The time after work, especially on a weekend, was spent improving the house. As soon as our container arrived with our household goods, life began to normalise. This time the container was delivered and lifted off the truck into a spot on the side of the house, where we wanted it.

At work, I was told to do extra hours, which helped our start. My normal income was rather low, but we had to start from somewhere, give our best shot and see what transpired.

In a small, highly efficient workplace like this one, everybody's task was diverse, because efficiency required multiple skills in an environment of skill shortage. I enjoyed my work with this company. The only question that was not answered to my satisfaction, was the pay. I had never worked on such a low pay as this. Excessive hours of work, including on weekends, was not the answer. Very soon, I could see a problem coming out of this situation. On the other side, the two owners showed off their business success with racing cars and a huge boat in its own special building. I am not denying those two owners their success—they were typical self made business people 'toughing it out' their way and why should somebody else have it easier than they had? Conveniently, they did not admit that they were also drawing off the experience of others. To coin a phrase, 'a jug makes its way to the well only until it breaks'. As I was put in charge of the technical side, which I appreciated, I also had to endure the difficulty of recruiting experienced technical staff. I made the point that we could not expect anything in return, if we did not offer anything. Specific attitudes like working with high precision for example require special experienced staff; pressure on staff does not necessarily make good people stay.

Our home in northeast Perth, Western Australia

With time, I managed to get a young tradesman from New Zealand onboard in our high-tech tool room section. He produced consistently fruits of his own mind, which unfortunately regularly ended in mistakes. I left the door open for him to join us in a more team-oriented approach. Just when I thought I had eventually brought him in line, he dropped out as a result of an accident with his motor- bike on an intersection. The day had just started without Marc, when two police officers turned up in my department, bringing with them the news that Marc had run a set of traffic lights and was hit by a crossing car. His condition was very serious.

His dreams for life were finished, we lost a good technical person, no replacement for him was on the horizon. This accident turned out particularly bad, because of the road condition in winter. In summer, it usually did not rain for a long time and minute oil residues from traffic often created a dangerous film on the surface of the roads around Perth. Once the drizzly weather season of winter began, the roads become extremely slippery. On a day like that, it was evident that Marc could not even have attempted to slow down when he crossed the intersection in a hurry facing red lights, and this so close to the company. We were all touched by this horrific accident, however, life had to continue.

The cold nights of this winter eased slowly during spring, in the months of September up to November.

On a weekend, when I didn't have to work and purchases in nearby shopping centres were effected, our family headed for the beach. Under the protection of a sand dune, we established our camp. We always had to walk a distance from the nearby road through an ocean of wild f lowers, carrying with us what we needed. The f lowers sprang up with the rain during winter. Their colours, the green; everything looked so fresh in this sand. It is difficult to comprehend how plant life in such abundance rises from sand. The wild f lower season in Western Australia is unique; it is not matched in its diversity anywhere in the world. I have seen the wild f lowers of spring in the Cape Province of South Africa and a very rare view of it in the Atacama Desert of Chile, although they do not produce this diversity.

Prehistoric times have prepared plants in Western Australia that have adapted to poor soil conditions. I took many pictures with my camera. The appearance of various grasses, spread in between f lower fields, is of special interest to a serious observer. During summer, this natural magnificence disappears, but what it left behind is an immense harvest of seeds, that present to our eyes each year such colourful unexpected splendour.

The summer of 1982/1983 had temperatures in Perth climbed to their extremes. We could not believe that children at school had sports during the day with temperatures reaching forty-seven degrees Celsius in the shade. At such high temperatures, the humidity stayed fortunately lower, which aided survival.

Family beach on a Sunday, Perth

West Australian beach, wild flowers

A phenomenon of Western Australia are its flies, mainly during summer. On special days, when the wind blows from northeast out of the Gibson Desert, trillions of black flies line up in a black band on the beach, just where the water spills onto the sand. These flies absorb the water evaporation. Nobody dared to disturb them, the beach was then empty of people—when those flies were on the beach, they created a nuisance for everybody.

The German shepherd, which shared our family life, suffered terribly with his ears from the flies. During the summer, the flies had eaten half of the dog's ears and left them in a terrible condition. Nothing was preventing them from also biting us and taking

a little piece of meat, so particular attention had to be paid to the danger of infection through the flies. They are always after the liquid substances in eyes. Aborigines have developed eye diseases from there. Those who have not experienced the flies of Western Australia on their special days, cannot comprehend such a plague. These flies are tough Aussies; having been around here longer than us, nothing stands in their way.

In the beginning of 1983, a family from Germany also tried their luck in Western Australia. They had our address and joined us for a while. On their day of arrival, we wanted to go with them to our favourite beach in the north of Perth. As we arrived with the car, we saw from inside of the car this black band of flies on the edge of the sea, but no fly elsewhere. As soon as we stepped outside, a swarm of flies suddenly surrounded each one of us aggressively, starting first in our faces. We returned quickly to our car and headed back home. Our friends were stunned by such a display of Australian nature.

On another occasion, when we stopped at a petrol pump on a tour in the outback, the only visible sign of human settlement was the accommodation carved into rock formations, as its name of Barry Caves indicated. A woman in shorts approached our car. Her legs and arms were black. On a closer look we realised, black flies covered her. I opened the window of the car to talk to her, flies from somewhere else were immediately on the scene to welcome us. I did manage to ask this lady how she coped with the pest and she replied, 'Get used to it, or don't come here.' The only good thing about flies is, they are not a constant threat; only rain in summer brings them out but when this happens, these black flies from the outback of Australia create hell for everybody.

The boss' racing car went out for a number of races that sum- mer. Our team won only once, because the favourite yellow opponent dropped out with a motor defect. These races are amazing, one can almost predict what has to be done to get a car ready for another race. In the pursuit of a maximum performance, everything is pushed to its limits, including the driver. To overhaul a motor sets you back each time as little as 20 000 dollars and this is only if you can do such work yourself.

In addition to our normal work, many hours went into racing. The owner had no family, which is why he had the spare time for racing. In Australia, many dream of races with a performance car. Many take this challenge, which they pursue with determination; but naturally only few make it. I must admit, I also experienced this racing fever, but I became critical about the time that went into it. The boss stuck to his guns, telling me, 'You work for me; you have to work on the racing side as well.'

The road to our company continued in a dead straight line for a couple of kilometres. This fact created a challenge one day—who could clock the highest speed on that road and turns at maximum speed into the yard of the company. The competitors were Kevin and Shane, both in his own racing car. They met the target with a great deal of a risk. It did not take long however for the roaring of racing engines to alert the police. When they turned up, they had in their mind to confront the drivers, our two bosses, for exceeding the speed limit, indicated on this road as sixty kilometres, as they had achieved three hundred kilometres per hour. The police looked very serious first, but Shane found a way to restore calm—each policeman was given the chance of their life, to drive a racing car themselves! Believe it or not, speed limits were forgotten. At the end all smiles returned, nothing serious was left behind.

Christmas time became an occasion where the company invited staff and their partners to dine in the city of Perth. The year gone by looked so very much different from that perspective, everything appeared from a bright side, which is what such occasions are for.

Banksia flower, Western Australia

Eucalypt flowers, Western Australia

I clocked one year with the company before the middle of the year and found it appropriate to ask for a review of my basic income. My request fell on deaf ears. I was told, 'You earn good money with the overtime, you won't find another job here in Perth.'

The owner began to make his view clear, 'tough out' his views. My learning curve in Australia wouldn't stop there. Generally speaking, manufacturing in Western Australia was still in its early beginnings, only a few enterprises stood out, like our company. Everybody was to a certain degree his own master. At work, we had a number of successful projects behind us. Another project turned up, where a copying model for a large injection mould was done outside very cheaply. Instead of firm solid contours, fibreglass mat was used to create the contours. The job started began with big problems; the computerised machine tool lost the contour each time the automated stylus dived through the weak fibreglass. I also knew that the positive shape would not fit the negative. As a result, the job ended up 'miles out', but no discussion was permitted on that matter. Instead, I found myself pushed more and more because time allocated for the project was running out. Work on weekends even with the help of my eldest son could not fix the problem in due time. This was going nowhere, I handed in my notice. I was told that there was no work for me in Perth and then asked where else could I go. My reply was that I would go back to where the work was. The decision was made; a new chapter in an migration effort was unfolding.

I am not denying that I had also to learn about the Australian way of work life, which is different from what I knew. I was firm and secure enough to keep looking for reasonable employment somewhere else. These are situations that a migrant might face during the first years.

Let me mention beforehand, it took me six years to find a reason- able, good job. This is not much out of a common understanding here in Australia of 'A migrant must learn to crawl first, before he can walk in Australia.' There is an unwritten rule, based on Australian experience—the first three years are the hardest, hardly anyone will listen to you. After five years, a migrant is on his way, cautiously he starts to participate in Australian life and can expect more of a wider acceptance in return. A complaining migrant cannot expect in the beginning to be heard, if you 'battle your way', you gain respect. Everybody's life in Australia started out small; life in Australia has never been easy, especially in the past. Nobody here is prepared to give you something, unless you deserve it. As long as a migrant keeps battling and doesn't give up, he will get somewhere, according to his real capabilities.

Contrary to traditional employment methods in Europe, a person can find their feet after a mishap much more quickly in Australia, when he tries hard enough.

As I pointed out earlier, all these comments might appear insignificant; each migrant experiences his own course of events. There is nothing bad in it, nor anything to be ashamed of. We all can only learn from one another with an open mind.

Kimberley road, northwest Australia

Termite mound near Broome

The year in Perth took too much time away from my family and we decided that there must be a better balance between work and family life; we were determined to look for this somewhere else. The family was again united in a decision to return to Queensland. Nothing was really lost; we were one Australian experience richer. It did not appear practical to go back the same way we had travelled to Western Australia a year ago. The alternative route would be through the north of Australia, 10 000 kilometres of Australian wilderness, very few human settlements on this way, great distances in between. As we entered the start of winter, we knew from reliable information that this was also the only time of the year that one could successfully drive through the north of Australia. This tour promised to become something like an expedition. I had to pay special attention to our Holden panel van. Nobody could afford a breakdown in the wrong place during such a tour. A respectable number of car parts came with us; a good tool selection was also vital.

As our container left with all our household goods for storage in Perth, we started our tour to Queensland through the north of Australia. Food, water, extra petrol, basic medicines, and Australian country music, was onboard with us. The children had their favourite toys and books in the car to bridge the hours of driving for the next two to three weeks. Everybody was exited, our very special sightseeing tour got under way in perfect sunny weather.

As soon as we left Perth, we found ourselves surrounded by wheat farming land. We had to give the natural sights of interest a miss in the south this time. During the year in Perth, we had not been able to spare the time to explore more of the wider area and now was not the time to do so. We were better focussed on a tour, one that brought us to Queensland without becoming side tracked by too many other things of interest. The road near the coast had very little traffic. Carnarvon grows the bananas of Western Australia and the plantations dominated the landscape. We experienced a substantial rise in temperature later in Port Headland, close to forty degrees Celsius mainly during the day. We shouldn't forget that this was winter! The dry season here turned the grass near the coast into brown and yellow colours. The Australian bush maintains its green and shoots a colourful blossom display in the midst of the dry season. No tree makes it in a rugged terrain of rock, red soil, yellow Spinifex grass and visibly exposed mineral deposits of iron-ore and copper.

After Port Headland, we entered the plains of the Great Sandy Desert, where destructive cyclones pass every summer season. Even the Australian bush finds survival problematic in that area, where a dust cloud on the horizon indicates an approaching road train, or stockmen on horse moving their cattle. In both cases, a driver is better off stopping on the side of the road to let the dust cloud pass. Road trains with their number of trailers behind move at high speed, their trailers can move on these stone–dust roads sideways. In a dust cloud, they become invisible for an oncoming vehicle. Serious accidents happen during such encounters. Not much better is the encounter with a herd of cattle.

Road cattle-train, outback Australia

Gibson Desert/cyclone area

That day, we finished at Sandfire Roadhouse. The sun had gone down already; the heat of the day did not ease at all though. The air was so hot, humid and still, the temperature was well over forty degrees. We had to rent an air-conditioned block unit in this settlement, if we wanted to sleep at all. The famous black flies also called this area home, which was one more reason to seek proper accommodation for the night.

The next day, we took the side trip to Broome, on the Indian Ocean, in the hope of gaining some relief from the heat. No relief happened, on the coast the humidity still increased. Tourist brochures don't tell about flies, heat and sultriness! No wonder that the Chinese were the only early settlers here, their steadfastness is a well-known fact. (It was the Chinese who began the pearl fishing industry here, which is still going under their rule.)

Very few tourists were seeking the shallow waters of the beaches to cool down. We preferred to rest a couple of hours in the shade of a huge fiddle-fig tree with its mass of large dark green leaves. The temperature of forty-two degrees even under the fiddle-fig tree did not invite us to stay any longer. Our road went inland to the Kimberley region, one of the most isolated areas in the world.

A few weeks earlier, we heard on the news in Perth about heavy floods in the Kimberley region. The first indication to this event was that large sections of the road ceased to exist; the whole structure of the road had been washed away. The bush on the side indicated the path of a previous bitumen road, which was now turned into a red, dusty, beaten track.

Rocky hill formations stood out of this ancient landscape, boab trees resist harsh weather conditions for thousands of years. The moisture stays with the heat in the air, day and night. It sometimes takes years for this moisture to develop into a deluge.

Washed away Kimberley road

Ancient Boab surrounded by termite mounds

Between Kununurra and Lake Argyle

Lake Argyle, Kimberley

The presence of the striking boab tree leads to a strong indication of an ancient connection with continents including Madagascar and Ecuador. In both countries, you can find forest structures of succulents with boab, the transition from dry country to rainforest.

Boab trees tolerate salt water, which is an indication that they adapted through history to changes in nature like sea level rises into the region. The look of an ancient boab is fascinating; its huge bottle-formed grey–brown trunk, the wild crown of twined branches carries relatively small and few green leaves, these trees look back into ancient history. Nobody knows whether a boab would live forever, if nature did not take its toll on it. Very little is known about them, Australia is still an ancient living museum through its landscapes, its botanical and zoological living forms, a widely unexplored paradise.

Driving for most of the day on dust, stone and the occasional bitumen roads, we had encounters with f locks of wild birds. They were hanging in the air above the heat over the road. As I came closer, the birds, mainly galahs, did not move out of their intended air route. I had to stop and let the birds have their passage first. What an encounter!

These birds were obviously not used to traffic and did not respond at all. We can call this unspoilt nature.

Arriving at Fitzroy Crossing, we learned at the local police station just how dramatic the floods had been only a few weeks ago. The Fitzroy River passes through a narrow passage at the crossing. Up on the hill from the police station, the river could not be seen anymore. And yet, this river was passing through the police station, which a water level stain halfway up in the room clearly indicated. Any unlucky traveller, who happened to be caught by this deluge, disappeared. Australia loves the extremes through its nature. This is something that everybody who lives in this part of our world has to be aware of.

The Ord River changed the arid Kimberley region into rich farming country of predominantly rice fields. Trees took foothold again and everything was lush and green.

In Kununurra, we branched off to Lake Argyle, a huge artificial water reservoir, the dam wall extending raised water levels far into the country. On the way to this lake, massive rock formations ran on a colourful inclination down to the road. The shiny surface of the lake interrupted those formations. For the first time since leaving Perth, we found a place crowded with people. They came with tents, caravans to holiday on the lake's shores. Straight after the huge curved dam wall, the riverbanks dropped deep down to the riverbed that continued from the lake. High up from the road it could not be missed—we saw crocodiles moving in and out of the water. This was a strong reminder to leave them alone.

After I had been at Lake Argyle, I got hold of an article about this area. This artificial water reservoir had been declared a biological time bomb. The reasons given were that water storage of such dimensions in an extreme temperature area with uneven precipitation, favoured bacterial growth, which under natural conditions was in balance with living forms. This balance is heading towards change and will endanger existing living forms. The introduction of a form of malaria has already happened. Hopefully a balance will prevail through unexpected positive natural forces of adaptation.

Coming back to Kununurra, we were only a short distance away from an artificial borderline of Western Australia. Somebody in England or Australia must have made this border decision with a stroke of a pen as the borderline ended up on the longitudinal degree of 129. This is the only single straight borderline of a territory in Australia. No wonder that Western Australia regards itself with its largest territorial size, a separate part of Australia. There is a traditional competition between the states of this continent, not only to their benefit, but also to some disadvantages.

Raging bushfires, Northern Territory

Sunset outback Australia

Larimah caravan park, Northern Territory

Three Ways on Stuart Highway

Outback Queensland pub

The grill of rails over the road shook every driver in his car and reminded to look at a sign on the roadside that welcomed with Northern Territory Outback Australia. What is this part of Australia claiming now in the competition of the states? They do not want to be called a state, they are a territory. Under this name, they found a clever combination within the state's families of Australia. They are on the receiving side of Canberra, but they decide their own affairs; in other words, they do not want to be told what to do by a centralised authority.

This northern part of the Territory is tropical. In summer, extreme temperatures produce heavy rain seasoned with regular destructive cyclones. With its high grass, the land around us showed the explosive growth during summer. During the months of winter, most of this vegetation turns brown, yellow and black, because of this prolonged dry season. Bush fires are quite common then. A driver has to watch very carefully these events, particularly how fires move in order to stay on the safe side. Many plants in particular in the Outback of Australia depend on fire for their own propagation. It is beyond doubt, however that there are many more fires accidentally or deliberately started through human civilisation, than through natural causes like lightening strike. A high number of fires could offset the balance in the Australian nature. The dense dry grasslands burn very quickly and intensely, leaving a trail of destruction behind, mainly in the 'specialised' animal world of this continent. Where the fire has turned the land black, the new fresh green of the cycads stands out dramatically from the black seemingly dead nature. Next summer, with the rain, life returns.

The main purpose of our tour was to get back to Queensland, although there was no harm in exploring and becoming acquainted with this special continent. Own knowledge with own experience helps towards a better identity with a country and its conditions.

There are plenty of new arrivals in this country that have hardly stepped outside the area of their arrival; I am not one of them. Some people deal with their insecurity through restricting themselves to a small area, others break down insecurity with a drive for knowledge. From there it also involves a fundamental difference with people, either settling in a country or visiting it only.

The next bigger township we passed was Katherine. A typical country town with one main road, where on both sides of it, all that a country town had to offer took place. At its entrance from the north, a bridge crossed the river with the same name of the town. What is quite obvious is how deep the water of this river flows between the rocks; an indication of how mighty during summer this present minute flow of water could become.

Whilst doing our shopping in Katherine, we noted the high percentage of indigenous Aborigines here who call Northern Territory their home, more so than other parts of Australia, their appearance is here more 'original', because of a more natural environment. Their integration into a modern society proves to be a very difficult task for Australia. The next kin to the Aborigines is to be found in remote areas of Papua New Guinea, a very old indigenous culture. Testimonies of their culture go back to 60 000 years in Kakadu National Park. Once again though, unfortunately we couldn't spare the time to explore more the detailed parts of the Northern Territory, which are of particular interest.

Our tour continued to the south, more into the Outback of this Territory. Mataranka, a tropical oasis, is the door to the Outback. A sunburned land, where nature constantly battles the elements for survival. Time has permanently marked the land with little or no water, soil has disappeared, rock has taken over, grass is most of the time dry; the Australian bush calls this home, a special animal world lives there, poverty and wealth coexist in nature. Nothing reveals its existence to the blind visitor; everything hides in the relative safety of nature, only revealing itself to the cautious, patient and unprejudiced visitor.

As the land on our way turned increasingly arid, Larrimah presented a surprise at the time. This small township on the Stuart Highway basically consists of two caravan parks, which are in opposition to one another. One of them stands out with a colourful magnificent garden. The entrance marks a huge bougainvillea with its dense red f lowers. For their efforts, the owners received the price of the most beautiful place in the Territory, this in a semi-desert environment! What this demonstrated is the fact that if somebody combined efforts with water, paradise can be created, but only when efforts are continued. Years later, when I came back there, I could not see paradise anymore; the place was regrettably run down.

Further on our way, wild bushfires forced us to stop for a while, until the f lames did not cross the road anymore. While we waited a safe distance from the fire, we could observe eagles cruising behind the f lames above the smoke in the air. The eagles waited for their moment to pick 'grilled wildlife' out of the ashes, wildlife that could not make the escape from the fire.

We found the roads in the Northern Territory in a surprisingly good condition. This fact plus its low traffic should not induce a driver to less attention. The only part of Australia to do so, the Territory had no speed limit outside of its cities. The consequence of this was that people make use of this freedom. An accident usually turns out to be a complete disaster, when it happens, perhaps due to the fact that there is much in the way of wildlife and the encounter with a kangaroo is more likely to be fatal for both driver and kangaroo.

For those that can read, the territory has put up road signs pledging for help to prevent fires: 'We want our lizards frilled, not grilled.'

Double storey, multi-trailer road trains also drive throughout the area on full speed. The vacuum they leave behind can suck a vehicle from oncoming traffic off the road very easily. High-speed traffic in the territory requires careful attention.

Our Holden had deserved praise, driving us almost around Australia without giving us any problems, which was very important. Own thorough maintenance, spare parts included in a tour, all this can be understood as insurance, which is good to have, even if it is not needed.

At Three Ways just before Tenant Creek, we left the Stuart Highway. As the name implies, one way went from there to the north to Darwin, a second way continued to the south to Alice Springs; the third way, our way, headed east to Queensland. The weather remained just fine; we saw neither one cloud in the sky nor one drop of rain with 6 000 kilometres behind us. This could also be called an Australian experience and certainly at the right time.

Huge cattle properties occupied the grasslands between Three Ways and Camooweal, the border town of Queensland. We could see only one property from the road with its typical setup of a farmhouse in the midst of shade trees, the only trees around.

Other properties announced the name of the homestead at an entrance from the road marked with timber posts at a surprising distance apart. On one occasion, the distance to a homestead was indicated as being 186 kilometres from the start of the property on the road.

A dust road usually leads to a homestead. Post is delivered once a week at the entrance on the highway in a milk bottle hanging horizontally on its own timber post, next to the entrance. In 2001, we took the opportunity to pay a visit to a homestead in the Northern Territory. We met people of distinct characters and experienced a very special atmosphere. The people in the harsh countryside of Australia are quite different from the population in the big cities; nowhere else did we experience such a fundamental difference in a population. The cities do waste resources, in the country is nothing to waste; this difference forms amazing characters in its people, they all make the population of Australia. The road condition told you, where Queensland started.

In the Northern Territory we left the good road behind; Queensland welcomed us on a dirt road through bushland. The State appeared at the time to have little interest to connect to other parts of Australia with its roads. This is another indication of a problem, which Federalism in Australia is facing, bringing the States together to unanimous decisions, towards the problems of federalism in Australia.

We find people in Australia on good terms with time, who won't be pushed: what can't be done today can wait a bit longer, but it will eventually happen.

The small township of Camooweal told the number of its permanent residents with a sign at the entrance. All these places suffered from an exodus mainly of the younger generation. This is why the population there is on the decrease. The land in the Outback offers very limited opportunities, only determined and tough people can make a living there.

After a good night's sleep in the local caravan park, our tour continued in Queensland. Next destination was Mount Isa.

Our road continued in Queensland style—sometimes bitumen road, sometimes dirt. The 'tsar is also here so far away, everything takes time to reach distanced places', (a symbolic saying, as this was the case in Russia under tsar-rule).

A tall chimney announces from distance the mining town of Mount Isa, which is situated high up against a backdrop of mountain ranges. Black dumps with conveyor towers impose a view in front of a settlement of neat houses, all surrounded with small gardens. Mount Isa is classified as one of the richest mining areas in the world. People that work there in underground operations earn good money, but also under distinct conditions. The main issue being the climate. When we stopped just outside of Mount Isa to have a rest with a picnic, we received a taste of the conditions there. In recent days, unseasonable rain had brought out the f lies. The sticky weather and the f lies stopped us having our rest in the open air. A rest was not so much uppermost on the agenda since we had arrived in Queensland. The remaining 2 500 kilometres to Brisbane we wanted to tackle in the shortest time possible from now on. Learning about this country first hand through our tour, came to the point that it was enough for now.

'All this country is not going anywhere'; we should have time in years to come to explore more of our backyard.

The railway construction from the coast got underway then. We received a friendly salutation from the workforce, when our road passed close by. Mountain ranges with dense forest cover introduced us into the Dividing Ranges, which run from south to north all along the east coast of the continent.

As their name says, they are divided into three distinct ranges, a green coastline range, an interior range, and a dry range of the Outback.

Sugarcane fields near Townsville, Queensland north

Near Townsville, we experienced our first rain during this tour. The sugarcane stood high and dense along parts of the road to the south. This indicated that the summer in Queensland had been hot and wet again. The rivers carried masses of water, all running from the ranges towards the sea. A few passages were flooded from rivers.

Back in the Kimberleys of Western Australia, we came to the flooded passage of a dirt road. At first we could see a few cars not moving, in the middle of a current. They all were 4-wheel drives and one tried to pull out the other to the opposite bank.

Misplaced confidence leads to this: getting stuck and having to put up with heat and f lies for a good while. I stopped and only ten meters upstream, I found a shallow passage with hardly any stones in the way. People busy with their 4-wheel drives being stuck, could not believe what they saw when I passed with our panel van across to the other side of the current—the time taken to check a situation always pays. For the rest of our tour along the coast of Queensland, we paid a visit to frequently well-established caravan parks at the end of a touring day. This is a facility that is available over the whole continent; all have cooking facilities, showers, toilets, and all this was available for a reasonable fee of an average of ten dollars per night.

We left the rain in the north behind us. A brief stop in Mackay reminded us that we were back in Queensland with its stylish Queenslander houses and tropical gardens, not to forget the sticky humid air during summer.

Caboolture caravan park

Brisbane arrived in due time and we entered it from the north. A new chapter started for us; we now had to find housing and work again. One step at the time, no undue rush, this was how we decided to face our next future.

We made our first enquiry on the day of our arrival in a caravan park and we struck our first obstacle. We could have stayed the night in the caravan park, but our German shepherd was excluded. Nevertheless, a solution is never far away. In our case, a caravan park that also admitted dogs, was located thirty kilometres back where we came from, in Caboolture. And this was how it happened that we finally arrived in Caboolture.

At nightfall, we rolled into Caboolture Caravan Park, at the Bruce Highway turnoff. After a well deserved good night's sleep in a rented and fully furnished caravan, I started to look for work on the first day. In the north of Brisbane, I found work very quickly with a plastic- injection-moulding company. I did not hesitate and started the next day. I was aware that I had to start somewhere and see again what the future might hold. One problem solved, the next one was to find housing so that we could move out of the caravan park.

Our children actually enjoyed the few weeks we spent in the caravan park, we all met new people. One meeting in particular became the start of a lasting friendship; Ray lived with his wife Mii in the close community of our temporary accommodation.

They both came from New Zealand, Mii from Rarotonga in the Cook Islands. Ray had the pleasure of playing the big uncle for our children; sympathy was established on both sides. From that time on, we kept in touch regularly with one another.

We had to begin our search for housing in order to send our children to a school. The heavy rainy season during summer 1982–1983 continued well into the winter. An extraordinary rain depression from a cyclone flooded the whole area in less than two days. The river next to the caravan park raised many meters and inundated many caravans.

We found ourselves in the middle of an ocean. As a consequence, nobody could move and in my case, I could not even go to work for a few days. As soon as the rain eased, the water in the river went back into its original bed. Now began in earnest the general effort to dry up during brief appearances of the sun. People have a common under- standing in Australia that when difficult times strike, everybody is there to give a helping hand; this can be called an Australian tradition. It feels good to stay with such people shoulder to shoulder.

Our affairs kept moving, because we didn't leave many stones unturned. A rental house in a suburb of Redcliffe peninsula gave back our family home. Only after a couple of weeks, our life in Queensland had its new direction.

Besides our family of seven, our German shepherd and two white cockatoos took residence in the house in Clontarf. We had a complete house again for ourselves, even when it was rented, it very much sup- ported our family life.

At that time, Australia could offer such facilities like renting a complete house for an affordable price. Our life was back to normal when our container arrived after some unexplained delay from Western

Australia. Our boys shared their room with the two parrots. Besides all the fun with them, the parrots produced at first daylight and dawn a terrible noise like an alarm clock, which was their way to welcome a day and say goodbye to it. Our children met the requirements of a local school without any problems. In our view, the view of the parents, the school was rather more relaxed than demanding. We chose to look at this from a positive perspective—our children were easily acquainted with the school in Australia.

The proximity of the house to the beach on Moreton Bay gave us the possibility nearly every day, to walk this short distance across a few road intersections, which we generally did after I had returned from work. A relaxed beach walk with a swim to follow finalised our day, away from the noisy farewell habit of our cockatoos. Nobody in our neighbourhood ever approached us with any complaint regarding our two cockatoos. We also did not miss the opportunity to talk to the people about that issue. Their comments were of a very relaxed nature, saying that birds were all around, they are only natural.

Such friendly behaviour is not common everywhere in the world, as I experienced later on a business trip in Europe, mainly in Germany. I paid a visit to my hometown, to see how my parents were. Being on foot in one of the many narrow roads of this ancient town, the familiar sound of an Australian cockatoo struck my ear. I stopped and entered the building where the noise appeared to be coming from. The service person in a hardware shop confirmed willingly my enquiry on the obvious and unmistakable Australian parrot's call. I could see in the back yard a reasonable sized luxury birdcage with one only Australian cockatoo in it. Nothing had been spared to accommodate this bird in the cold climate of Germany. No wonder, when I heard how much had been paid for this cockatoo; which had to have been the Black Market price, because officially Australian birds are not exported for good reasons. The noise of the cockatoo developed into a problem very quickly, in this densely populated area. People demanded to be rid of what they termed a nuisance. This happened very quickly then the birdcage remained empty and silent. This situation fortunately did not happen to us in Australia. Certainly, not every 'Aussie' will fit into an environment in Germany.

Our life was finally running at a good pace, a change at work was not waiting to happen. I arrived at work like every other day, when the boss had the news for me that he had no more work, that I had done well and when needed again, he would let me know. 'Here is your pay, thank you,' he said; I simply was stunned about what I had just heard. I said to myself that if this was the case, let us move on, there must be other opportunities. What touched me with a strange feeling, was the fact that the boss also came from Germany, but never spoke a word of German with me.

I did not hesitate to seek other opportunities; there was no use in remaining upset about what had happened; this should be left in the past. My learning curve continued to rise in Australia.

The second Aussie, our son Michael, joined our family in July 1984. The family was now strong enough for Australia.

I was under no illusion that it would take more time for me to test the local labour market for a position; that would also suit me. During that process, I remembered a company that I had an interview with more than a year ago. Despite the fact that they had moved away from the city into new premises, I knew I could track them down. Their interest was still current, so we reached an immediate agreement to get me started the next day. The travel distance from home to work and back became a minor issue in front of the work conditions I was offered at least in the beginning; engineering tooling design work was my own responsibility including the fabrication

Everything went to satisfaction for both sides. Before the end of a year, a gentleman started his employment mainly in the area of the company's administration. He vowed to 'cut my wings' in my independent operation within the company, wanting total control. I offered my cooperation to give this new level of politics no cause for disagreements. Everything continued to work on a reasonable level. One day however, as I performed more and more design work for the company, I found *my* drawings bearing the signature of this gentleman. I asked him the question how was it that he is signing for what I am doing and that he could approve it if he wanted. He knocked me firmly on the head and replied, 'If you work here from now on, you do what you are told.' I agreed on what he asked for, but the atmosphere started to become tense. Around that time, on the weekends mainly, we were looking for suitable land to buy. Still today, there is no shortage of land to buy in Australia; this has to be one of the biggest real estate markets in the world. We looked outside of the city for a bigger block of land with a view that we preferred to visit a city instead of having the city around us day and night. We had experienced how quickly developments of a city can interfere with private interests during our years in Brazil. Australia is not Brazil with its development speed; everything is still on a slower pace of development. Land prices were at that time very cheap in comparison with Europe. Our choice ended up in the Shire of Caboolture, outside a small country town with public transport to Brisbane, the highway to Brisbane also in close proximity.

According to our wishes, we found a rural piece of land the size of one hectare and we were not yet cut off from the rest of the world— such a choice had to be made very thoroughly. The land is on a very slight inclination to drain the heavy summer storms.

As the name 'Green Meadows' indicates, there are mainly grasslands, where pumpkin farming was done for a number of years. The soil of this land was of particular interest to me, when I realised how loose and black this soil was, our decision became quickly cemented. The land was sitting on a reef of lava streams from the nearby extinct ancient volcano formations of the Glasshouse Mountains; in other words, a land with very fertile soil.

We had remembered the advice of the immigration authorities, which was to call on a proper solicitor to deal with property transactions on our behalf. To do so, I asked at work for two days off duty. With the formalities over, I returned to work to find out that the gentleman took the opportunity to sack me during my absence. I could not believe this; he didn't even have the guts to tell me this in person. What a fine response to our move to be settled. Hiring and firing of staff was at that time in Australia a common practice; no wonder that the country had a serious shortage of qualified people. A Labor Government turned this practice around into a new unbalanced problem in years to come, staff could not be sacked at all anymore.

You may ask why I write about occurrences as they happened to us? I have the strong view to communicate here with readers to pass on messages as true as possible, to promote a realistic understanding. Nothing is really bad, it just happens. Perhaps the lesson to be learned is to keep oneself moving in a new country like Australia. A person who claims not to have any problems, will face his future with uncertainty, when the question arises, whether or not he is experienced enough to tackle problems in his life.

In our case, as a family, we had learned a new lesson—let us keep going. No matter which angle you look at a migration from, the existence of a breadwinner in a family involves going through difficult stages before any settlement is reached. It is also important for that reason to realise, migration is not a way to get rid of problems; there is only a shift in problems. It ultimately depends on which package one gets used to.

If somebody capitulates in the face of problems through migration, they will not necessarily change that course in a new country. Some learn under new conditions, others never learn. There are personal conclusions I arrived at in relation to other migrants over the course of many years. Such experience indicates to me that all problems usually relate to only a few causes.

This element of living with problems makes the 'true blue Aussie': 'an Aussie, who has settled successfully for three generations in the country', (according to their own definition). In Australia I found people leaning towards 'near enough is good enough'.

Europe on the other side tends more towards perfectionism, because of competition on a much larger scale. 'Perfect people' put themselves under more stress than 'near-enough people', because as nobody is perfect, the constant demand to achieve perfection in life, can create a more of an uneasy personality. Whereas our 'near-enough' character avoids the personal conflict with the demand attached to perfectionism. In the Australian industry however, one would like to see more of the discipline towards perfectionism, international trade exchange demands it. As we well know, we can't have it both ways.

The kindness, the readiness to help, which even foreigners experience in Australia, is reason enough to accept the Australian way of life, which is sometimes also expressed through an easier approach of 'near enough is good enough'. This should not mislead—the Australian way of life also begs balance in hard work, through relaxation and in a community sense. Everybody in Australia is asked to produce not the 'perfect' Aussie but the Aussie, who battles his way through life best with his mates.

Where were we left after an unexplained dismissal from work (which I must say, never happened before to me)?

After one door closed, we had to keep our eyes peeled for another open door. Looking in the local newspaper for job vacancies, I found one for me. An international company sought a design engineer in manufacturing.

I fortunately had a telephone connection already on my land, outside Caboolture; I could be contacted and was able to respond. The interview went better than I could have expected. I was asked to start immediately and for the first time, my remuneration very good. A reason to celebrate at home; I had for the first time the feeling that I made it. The work was of interest, I did my best to fit into this engineering department team. Everybody came from a different part of the world and a nice working atmosphere united this team as a result.

Chapter 4

Life Stabilises

While the working week claimed most of my time for this new job, our weekends were spent working towards plans to build our own house. Confidence started taking a foot-hold in our lives. Our home was to become our castle. Every available minute went into it, especially in the first twelve months, until we could move from the caravan into the house that was finished in the rough.

When we started on our land, summer 1985 was also hot and wet. For that reason, we had to accommodate ourselves in a caravan that we could still live in comfortably. This was achieved with the construction of a protection roof over the caravan, annex, shower, our container and the entrance area. Water, power and the tele- phone were at that time supplied to rural areas with substantial subsidy under the Premier Bjelke-Petersen, which became welcome assistance for us.

Temporary set-up on own rural property near Caboolture

The small garden around our provisional caravan site gave the look of a beautiful setting, even though it was small. A school bus also serviced our area to take the children to a school in Caboolture at eight am. and return them by four pm. This system is designed to help families in the country with the education of their children; it was free of charge in certain areas and operated quite reliably. All schoolchildren wear uniforms specific for each school in Australia. Such standard provides an equal footing for every student in an education effort.

Life on our land started to turn in a promising direction. In order to build our own house, I managed to receive an owner builder's licence. Nothing in this world ever goes without problems, and so our building project followed suit. The local building inspector did not know me, which I believe to be the reason some problems crossed our way, but nothing that could not be resolved.

At work, the technical manager who had appointed me resigned, hinting to me that major changes in the company were on their way.

Not long afterwards, everybody in the company knew exactly what these changes were.

Decisions had been made overseas to shut down the operation in Queensland. Two weeks before Christmas we had this all in writing, attached was the final pay, Christmas and New Year wishes not forgotten. The unwanted part of this operation-shut-down was the success of the Queensland company in becoming opposition for the overseas operation.

This, the first peak period of my professional ambitions in Australia, lasted just one year, when we were sent back to start anew.

International businesses claim today that everybody's job has to be on a flexible basis, Australia would very much be a front-runner in this requirement. At least I had experienced good working conditions in this past year. It would have been of no use to complain; rather we chose to continue in the search for something similar.

Small, controlled steps in our private life paid off in advance of such an unforseen event. We did not owe anybody anything and therefore we could still secure our achievements on our property. For a number of weeks we worked extensively on our house, before I decided to look for new employment. In order to get us moving, I accepted a number of jobs for a short period of time; even gave it a trial in Melbourne.

Working conditions were less of an 'agricultural' approach there, than was the case for Brisbane. The sheer size of Melbourne and the much higher property prices determined our future in southeast Queensland.

The day arrived when I found an advertisement in a Brisbane newspaper, which I followed up and an interview was arranged. The company reflected a rather modest operation at that time. The owner however, pointed towards an interesting future. 'We have started manufacturing air-conditioning systems for cars, we are operating today mainly in the aftermarket with a plan to supply original systems from our factory to the Australian car industry, if you can help us, you've got a job.'

Before I accepted this job offer, I categorically referred to a remuneration figure under which I was not prepared to work. The owner shook hands with me, replied with his idea and asked, 'How do you like this? ' I could only accept with pleasure.

The place where I worked accepted my request for leaving at short notice. The owner of the new place offered his cooperation, because I had started with very little in the way of existing technical materials—a challenge I liked.

Work for the company from outside stopped immediately with my start. When the first projects came to a successful completion, the owner started with his plans for expansion. Firstly, a tradesperson was recruited to work with me. The boss spent quite some time with me, wanting to see for himself how I designed and made automated manufacturing equipment. Progress within the company happened then in big steps.

House finished in raw, 1986, Caboolture, Queensland

Professional confidence returned, I was happy with this employment, I could see a future. And I was not wrong; after just six months in the job, the owner took me to Hong Kong and Taiwan to buy new machinery.

Before this event, I made a decisive step to adopt Australian citizenship. Sooner or later, such a decision has to be made, if somebody is serious about life in a new adopted country. In the ceremony a vow was made to the Queen; this was a formal necessity, which was a tradition in Australia that time. One could be critical about this, but tradition has never hurt anybody. Every piece of tradition has more of an importance in a new country like Australia, where tradition is still in the making by its people.

Everybody who comes to this country can bring his own customs, his own language, his own traditions, as long as he accepts to practice his part in tolerance with mutual respect towards others. The question arises very often, what can a migrant contribute to a multicultural society? The contribution of a migrant is also his identity, which becomes a vital part in a process of acceptance. This is the real test, whether somebody has customs, tradition or culture, which he is asked to produce. A lot of people decorate themselves with foreign feathers and in a migrant situation there are much less foreign feathers around to relate to.

You have something to identify yourself in customs, tradition, culture and knowledge, you have an entrance ticket into the Australian society; if you cannot produce this, an identity problem will haunt you and make acceptance and success much more difficult.

It is also a misunderstanding when migrants let their customs, tradition and culture slip away in their own language. Nobody requests that of you, this can be only classified as a personal impoverishment with all its accompanying consequences.

Finished house with large verandas around, Queensland style

I could call myself from now on an Aussie and be proud of it, like everybody else in the country. This symbolic step reassured others that after a period of time I can accept the Australian way of life. Indeed, for the trip to Hong Kong and Taiwan I was already in possession of an Australian passport. The way we focus on a new environment is the same way acceptance is returned, and only a positive attitude will prevail.

Acceptance does not happen overnight. Everybody needs time to step out of the past and accept a new future. This is a big step in life, especially since some countries like the country of my previous residence, Germany, abolishes its own citizenship by adopting another citizenship.

I personally have no regrets on that matter. Countries that abolish their citizenship, when another citizenship is acquired, should think twice before they lose touch with their own citizens. There are many countries around that prove dual citizenship is totally acceptable.

The first years on our property, summers were extremely hot and humid. Until I was able to consolidate the driveway on our property to our house, I regularly got stuck in mud with my car. The only way out was the land next to us, which was fortunately not occupied during that initial period of time. We experienced temperatures of forty-eight degrees Celsius in the shade. Work was going very hard at the time; the determination sometimes released unavoidable swear words. Our little daughter Gucki used to say, when the weather was more favourable, 'Mum, have a look outside, the weather is beautiful, no sun! ' Working conditions at that time couldn't be described better than this.

How strong the sun looks out of the sky, can be best experienced on typical Australian work situation like concreting, bricklaying, roofing and fencing. I haven't done these jobs by profession, but I got the message with what I had to do on my land. Only one who has experienced this himself, has understanding of it—clouds in the sky are motionless with the air, radiation of the sun breaks through, but cannot return. Such a condensation makes work in the open extremely hard. Only water over your head and into your stomach helps you to survive. I had never experienced such conditions before, neither in Africa, nor in South America, not to mention Europe. Concreting, bricklaying, roofing and fencing in a Queensland summer is not far from 'convict work'.

The connection of 'convict' with Australia could be seen more likely from this angle. I can tell you, somebody doing this work in Australia is anything but a convict, these people are vigorous and tough, they are also the real Aussies.

Part views of entrance from road, Caboolture, Queensland

Our life after six years in the country turned us toward regular activities; our children pursued their first goals through education.

The rural character around us helped us by virtue of the fact that the children did not go off on a common trend by too far. Also, children have to stand up outside home to become accepted, win friends, to achieve something for themselves. Life outside home as they should know, had to be different, especially if this was the home of a migrant family. There is no way around this process, the waves 'reach heights', but they also will come down. It all depends how firm the parents stay in such a modern battle—if we want our children to return home when they are adults, we have to accept that they also go away to find out how home really was. This ancient change of generation is intensified in the case of a migrant family. The lack of family connections in most cases can drive children away from the everyday habits of parents into other camps. Nobody can guarantee how children develop, today, there is a combination of luck and parents' efforts to succeed.

The natural preoccupation of migrant parents to achieve something in a new country of their choice, leads very easily to neglect within a younger generation. We tried to control this problem in that we asked the children to participate in the construction of our new life. They decided how much assistance at the time they wanted to give and we in return looked at the possibilities to reward them with what was in our power.

All in all, it worked most of the time, our family residence came along, the children played their role at school. The role of the mother in a migrant family deserves a special note: she is the one who creates the home atmosphere for all, so it is a pleasure to come home to find all the little things in order. The old way of thinking of a family life has still its meaning, yet sharing the task at home and outside, ensures that nobody's burden grows too quickly and home remains the place where everybody likes to come back to.

Chapter 5

- -

The Conclusion

It took us six years to find a direction in Australia, where we could start to build up. Nobody really can say whether this was a short or a long time. Considering the end result: I worked nineteen years successfully in one place until my retirement at the age of sixty-five, our children found their way in life, the residence was developed to a family treasure, everybody in the family remained healthy—all this is reason enough to be finally content and proud of success. Looking back, when all the good things in our life take over, the conclusion comes to hand that we made it in Australia.

The continuity to transform a very small business into an ultra- modern company with international reputation provided a number of bonuses to me and my family, in return for hard work. Slowly but steadily we could afford a better life through my income. Overseas trips kept me in contact with other parts of the world, besides its business nature, there was always the opportunity to catch up with family and long-established friends.

Returning to the country from where we migrated, it became evident

Part of our typical tropical Queensland garden

only then that they hadn't changed noticeably, but we have changed considerably during the years in Australia. Talking to friends, former acquaintances; they had different views of life than we have quietly adopted as migrants; they are more concerned about health, security and wealth. A possible reason for that is, a migrant must adapt to challenges relative to a new country, if success is a goal. Whereas 'back home', changes happen more as a last resort, when everybody *collectively* has to change. A migrant has to go back to where he came from, in order to find out about his changes; in Australia, this will not become evident. Only in a comparison between the two countries will he learn about his own changes. Quite a number of migrants express their doubts regarding their adopted country, because they are lacking this vital comparison. Firstly, it takes time to learn in a new country; therefore an unofficial figure of three to five years for the process of a settlement to begin to work, comes into consideration for a migrant. A critical migrant with less than five years 'migration battle' on his shoulders, is not considered a serious champion; all he needs though is more time to learn. Generally speaking, the Australian public understands a migrant, who is struggling on his way as I believe that everybody in this country has gone through something akin to hardship, even if not the same.

Within Australia, we undertook several well-planned tours to build on our personal experience. The more we learned, the more we realised how diverse and unique this ancient museum continent is. You will find here in Australia most landscapes of the world in one place, if the time is taken to look around long enough.

At sixty-five, my work life has changed over to writing—a circle going back many years is now closing. In conclusion, a query and a few thoughts for the reader:

Would you agree that this is an exceptional migrant experience ?

Remember, every migrant experience is individual. We can learn from other experiences for our own life. For my family and I, this was what migration was about.

Printed in the United States
By Bookmasters